BEAT NEG
WITH CBT

BULLET GUIDE

Hodder Education, 338 Euston Road, London NW1 3BH

Hodder Education is an Hachette UK company

First published in UK 2011 by Hodder Education

This edition published 2011

Copyright © 2011 Paul Jenner

The moral rights of the author have been asserted

Database right Hodder Education (makers)

Artworks (internal and cover): Peter Lubach
Cover concept design: Two Associates

British Library Cataloguing in Publication Data: a catalogue record for this title is available from the British Library.

10 9 8 7 6 5 4 3 2 1

The publisher has used its best endeavours to ensure that any website addresses referred to in this book are correct and active at the time of going to press. However, the publisher and the author have no responsibility for the websites and can make no guarantee that a site will remain live or that the content will remain relevant, decent or appropriate.

The publisher has made every effort to mark as such all words which it believes to be trademarks. The publisher should also like to make it clear that the presence of a word in the book, whether marked or unmarked, in no way affects its legal status as a trademark.

Every reasonable effort has been made by the publisher to trace the copyright holders of material in this book. Any errors or omissions should be notified in writing to the publisher, who will endeavour to rectify the situation for any reprints and future editions.

Hachette UK's policy is to use papers that are natural, renewable and recyclable products and made from wood grown in sustainable forests. The logging and manufacturing processes are expected to conform to the environmental regulations . the country of origin.

.w.hoddereducation.co.uk

eset by Stephen Rowling/Springworks

nted in Spain

BEAT NEGATIVITY WITH CBT

BULLET GUIDE

Paul Jenner

About the author

Paul Jenner writes about getting the most out of life. He is the author of more than 30 books including *Be More Confident*, *Transform Your Life With NLP* and *How To Be Happier* (all published in the Teach Yourself series by Hodder Education). He lives in Spain, between the mountains and the sea, with his partner, three ponies, two dogs and two sheep. He would be delighted to receive your comments on his website: www.pauljenner.eu.

Contents

Introduction

Which comes first, thoughts or feelings? The answer is … **thoughts**. That leads us to a concept that is both profound and yet very simple. If you endeavour to **stop thinking negative thoughts** and to **think only positive thoughts**, you'll feel more positive and become a more **positive person**. In the same way, if you try to **think only happy thoughts**, you'll feel happier and become a **happier person**. And the same is true for many other qualities. Your brain is 'plastic', that's to say, if you change your **cognitions** (thoughts), you can change the structure of your brain and change the way you feel. Permanently. But what happens if, try as you might, you *can't* change your thoughts? If you can't see that spider as harmless, the 30th floor as safe, or groups of fellow human beings as anything but intimidating? In that case, you may be able to **desensitize** yourself through **gradual exposure**, that's to say, change your **behaviour**, little by little. Put these two techniques together and you have the powerful combination that's known as **CBT – cognitive–behavioural therapy**.

1 What is CBT?

Cognitive–behavioural therapy (CBT) can solve certain **psychological difficulties** or simply help you lead a more **successful** and **satisfying** life. CBT is a combination of:

* cognitive therapy (CT) – which is based on the belief that the way you **feel** is due to your **thoughts** (cognitions)
* behavioural therapy – which is based on the belief that certain problems can be overcome by practical techniques such as **desensitization**.

The way you feel is due to your thoughts

So cognitive therapy and behavioural therapy are based on quite different ideas and take rather different approaches. Yet, in combination, as CBT, they work very well together. CBT has enjoyed several decades of success in adults and young people in a wide range of situations. In this chapter we will look at:

* the history of CBT
* the applications of CBT
* the principles of CBT
* the effectiveness of CBT
* how CBT is administered.

History of CBT

Dr Albert Ellis (1913–2007) was the pioneer of CBT. In 1957 he formally proposed that therapists should help clients adjust both their thinking *and* their behaviour. His two-step process, known as **rational therapy** (RT), began with logical analysis of a client's true situation, followed by work to change the client's outlook. **Dr Aaron T. Beck** (b. 1921) is considered to be the father of the narrower cognitive therapy, which emphasizes the power of thought alone. These ideas, however, go back for centuries.

> We are what we think.
> All that we are arises with our thoughts. With our thoughts we make our world.
>
> Buddha

Applications of CBT

CBT can be used for the treatment of various difficulties including:

* post-traumatic stress disorder (PTSD)
* obsessive–compulsive disorder (OCD)
* eating disorders
* anxiety disorders and phobias
* chronic fatigue syndrome/myalgic encephalomyelitis (ME)
* insomnia
* depression.

But you don't actually have to have any particular problems at all in order to benefit from CBT. You can also look upon it as a type of **positive thinking** that can be useful in life generally.

There is nothing either good or bad, but thinking makes it so.

William Shakespeare

Principles of CBT

Ask yourself, if someone insults you and you get angry:

1 Was it the other person who made you angry?

or

2 Was it you who made yourself angry?

CBT holds that *you* make *yourself* angry. That can be hard to accept at first. But when you think about it, other people cannot *make* you angry. It's your **cognition** – the way you perceive and reason – that results in your becoming angry. With a different way of looking at the world you might, for example, have laughed or simply have ignored the insult.

If your perception is accurate your emotions will be normal

6

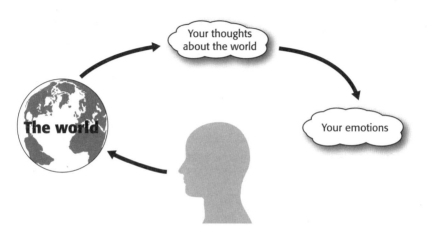

Your mood is created not by the world itself but by the way you **perceive** and think about the world. If your **perception** is **accurate,** your emotions will be **normal**. But if your perception is **inaccurate** and your thoughts **distorted** as a result, then your emotions will be **abnormal**.

Ask yourself, if a harmless insect that you're afraid of (let's say a spider) ran across the table in front of you, would you:

1 run out of the room in terror

or

2 force yourself to pick it up, smile, and put it outside?

If it's harmless, then you could indeed smile at the audacity of the little creature. This is the **behavioural** part of CBT. If you have an **irrational** fear, you can learn to overcome it step by step by **gradual exposure**.

For the treatment to be successful, it's not necessary to know *why* you have the fear. The important thing is to learn that you can overcome it.

For example, if you're afraid of heights you could begin by taking the lift to the first floor of a tall building and going out on to a balcony. Next day, go to a second-floor balcony. The following day go to the third floor. If that's difficult, keep returning to the third floor until you're relaxed. Then go up to the fourth floor. And so on. Eventually you will become more and more used to heights.

Effectiveness of CBT

Does CBT work? Various studies have found CBT to be effective.

CBT has been recognized by the World Health Organization (WHO) as best practice for the treatment of anxiety in children.

CBT has been recommended by the UK's National Institute for Health and Clinical Excellence (NICE) as the treatment of choice for various mental health problems including depression.

Computerized CBT (CCBT) was recommended by NICE in 2006 for the treatment of mild to moderate depression.

In a large-scale study in 2000, CBT, together with antidepressants, achieved significantly better results than antidepressants alone.

CASE STUDY

One group of patients was given antidepressants. Another group was given CBT. Positron emission tomography (PET) scans revealed that both groups experienced almost identical improvements in **brain chemistry** and architecture. However, the advantage for those in the CBT group was that they learned **skills** they could use throughout their lives, without recourse to drugs.

Administration of CBT

How can you receive CBT?

* on a one-to-one basis
* in a group
* via a computer
* self-help.

Even if you are receiving treatment from a professional, research shows that **self-help** is always key to making progress.

2 How to combat negative thinking

We all know about the glass that can be viewed as either half full or half empty. You'll be happier seeing the glass as half full, but both views are equally valid. Sometimes, however, **perception** bears little or no relation to the **truth**. You see the glass as only a quarter full, or even empty. This is thinking that is not only **negative** but also **distorted**.

You'll be happier seeing the glass as half full

CBT identifies ten different kinds of **distortions** that may need correcting if you're to enjoy a **happy** and **fulfilling** life. In this chapter we will look at:

1 all-or-nothing thinking
2 generalizing
3 focusing on the negative
4 ignoring the positive
5 magnifying and minimizing
6 jumping to negative conclusions
7 labelling
8 personalizing
9 'should' statements
10 emotional reasoning.

● CBT will help you enjoy a happy life

All-or-nothing thinking

If you see everything very much in terms of **black** and **white**, then you're committing the error of **all-or-nothing thinking**.

* I didn't win, therefore I'm a failure.
* I didn't get promoted, therefore I'm a loser.
* There's a mistake in this report, therefore the whole thing is worthless.

This way of looking at life is demoralizing and completely unrealistic. Nobody wins everything, most people never win at anything, nothing is perfect and one error doesn't invalidate an entire report. The answer is to allow some **grey** into your thinking – and also to **enjoy** what you do for itself, not for being first or best.

16

Generalizing

If you see one event as representative of everything or everybody, then you're making the mistake of **generalizing**.

✳ Being turned down for a date means that no one wants to be with me.
✳ My credit card has been stolen – you can't trust anyone.

The answer is to recognize that whatever happened is an isolated incident and does not signify anything about the wider picture.

TOP TIP
When you find yourself believing a generalization, test by seeing if you can prove the opposite.

Focusing on the negative

If you find yourself dwelling on a tiny hiccup in something that was otherwise perfectly successful, then you're making the error of **focusing on the negative**.

* If I hadn't missed that goal, we would have been five up instead of four up.
* I look so ugly with this mole on my face.

The opposite side of the coin is that you're **ignoring the positive**.

In a similar way, you may fall into the trap of **magnifying** problems and **minimizing** the significance of your achievements.

The answer in all these cases is to **reverse your mindset**. Focus on the positive and ignore the negative.

18

Jumping to negative conclusions

If you're often **jumping to negative conclusions,** then you're creating a great deal of unnecessary anxiety.

* You have a pain somewhere and immediately begin worrying about fatal consequences.
* You hear people giggling and feel sure they're laughing at you.
* You see your partner in intimate conversation with someone and assume you're being cheated on.

In human relationships, jumping to negative conclusions inevitably leads to negative behaviour, and that can be damaging. Don't do it. But if you do insist on jumping to conclusions on the basis of inadequate or incomplete evidence, then you'll be a lot happier if you jump to **positive** conclusions. Why not?

Labelling

Many people fall into the trap of **labelling** themselves and others.

* ❊ You don't get a job you wanted, so you label yourself a 'loser'.
* ❊ Some acquaintances disagree with your political views, so you label them 'bigots'.

These kinds of tags are simplistic and unrealistic but, once applied, they tend to stick. They blind you to everything else. Remember, you cannot define yourself or other people on the basis of one event.

● Don't use labels

Personalizing

If you assume responsibility for, and feel guilty about, problems that really have little or nothing to do with you, then you're making the mistake of **personalizing**.

✳ It's all my fault my father crashed the car; I should have stopped him driving before he got as old as this.

✳ It's all my fault my teenage son did so badly in his exams; I should have given him more help.

This kind of thinking takes no account of the fact that other people have to take responsibility for themselves. You cannot hold yourself responsible for other people's actions.

'Should' statements

On the previous page you may have noticed the word 'should'. When you feel guilty about not doing something, or irritable when other people haven't done something, then you're being overwhelmed by **'should' statements**.

* I should have known better.
* I should settle down.
* He should have acted sooner.

If you consistently adopt this style of thinking, then you're often going to be disappointed in yourself and other people. The answer is not to be so hard on people – and that includes you.

Emotional reasoning

Once you've generated negative emotions as a result of distorted thinking, they can become self-reinforcing. Because you feel bad you take this as evidence that everything truly *is* bad. This is known as **emotional reasoning**.

* I feel lonely – obviously nobody cares about me.
* I feel sad – clearly the world is a rotten place.
* I feel overwhelmed – undeniably my problems are insoluble.

The answer is to **challenge** these emotions and the thoughts that lie behind them.

A man's life is what his thoughts make of it.

Marcus Aurelius

3 How to increase self-esteem

Low self-esteem is at the root of a great deal of unhappiness. Demoralizing in itself, it also **magnifies** the **emotional impact** of all the distortions described in the previous chapter. If you do suffer from low self-esteem, the exercises in this chapter will help you. But don't just read about them. Make sure you also **practise** them regularly.

Low self-esteem is at the root of a great deal of unhappiness

It's a mistake to feel that your self-esteem should be related to what you perceive as your achievements or failures. On the contrary, it has nothing to do with your job or your bank balance. If you do suffer from low self-esteem, these techniques will **rapidly** and **significantly improve** it:

* talking back to your negative inner voice
* the three-column exercise
* the diary of negative thoughts.

● Self-esteem has nothing to do with your job or your bank balance

Talking back to your inner negative voice

Let's say you're about to attempt something difficult when a little voice tells you: 'You're not good enough.' Immediately your **confidence** is dented, and you just can't seem to operate at your **full potential**. Who would say such a demoralizing thing to you? The answer, of course, is yourself. We all have an **inner voice** that comments on what we're doing. If that inner voice is negative and critical, as is so often the case, then self-esteem is bound to suffer.

We all have an inner voice that comments on what we're doing

When your inner voice is negative the answer is to **talk back**. You could simply say:

✳ Shut up!

You could drown it out with a **positive message**:

✳ I have the necessary skills. I can do it. I *can*.

You could also engage in a debate:

✳ What's your evidence for saying that? Let's analyse it. After all, I've done similar things before …

● Tell that inner voice to shut up!

The three-column exercise

Talking back is a good technique to use at the moment a challenge arises. But, for habitual negative thoughts, the **three-column technique** is more powerful.

When you have a little time for reflection, take a sheet of paper and draw two lines down it to create three columns:

* Head-up the left-hand column 'Negative thoughts'.
* Head up the middle column 'Distortions'.
* Head up the right-hand column 'Realistic thoughts'.

Then fill the columns in.

Example of the three-column technique

Negative thoughts	Distortions	Realistic thoughts
Nobody likes me	All-or-nothing thinking/ generalization/ magnifying	It's just not true. There are one or two people who don't get on with me, but I actually have several good friends
Failing this exam means I'll never get on in life. I'm a loser	All-or-nothing thinking/ generalization/jumping to negative conclusions/ labelling	Failing one exam doesn't mean I'll fail at everything. That's ridiculous. I can always take the exam again or switch to something that suits me better. I've succeeded at plenty of things

Diary of negative thoughts

If you already keep a **diary,** this next idea will come easily.

* Whenever something happens that makes you feel bad about yourself, immediately describe it in your diary, together with the **thoughts** you had at the time.
* Score the **feelings** those thoughts created on a scale of 1–10.
* With the benefit of a little distance, **analyse** the situation to uncover the **distortions** in your thinking and to identify thoughts that would have been more **realistic**.
* When you've done all that, **finish** off by again scoring your feelings on a scale of 1–10.

Hopefully, your negative feelings will have become far less significant.

Example of the diary of negative thoughts

The situation	My boss shouted that I'd made a complete mess of everything
Thoughts at the time	I'm no good at this. I'll never succeed. I never do anything right. I'll get the sack
Feelings at the time (scale of 1–10)	Upset 8; inadequate 8; frightened 7; humiliated 9
Distortions	All-or-nothing thinking/generalizing/focusing on the negative/ignoring the positive/magnifying/jumping to negative conclusions/emotional reasoning
Realistic thoughts	I got one thing wrong. That's hardly making a 'mess of everything'. I've been perfectly successful recently, so I won't get the sack. My boss was in the wrong
Feelings now (scale of 1–10)	Upset 5; inadequate 1; frightened 4; humiliated 3

It can be very useful to recognize **how often** you have **negative thoughts** during the day. If you knew, the total would probably astonish you. Let's try to find out.

Every time you notice that you have a negative thought, **record** the fact in some way. You could draw a minus sign in a notepad, or key an N (for 'negative') into the memo facility of your mobile phone, or even use a wrist counter. At the end of each day, add them up and record the number in your diary.

34

If the doors of perception were cleansed, everything would appear to man as it is ...

William Blake

Once you've established your general daily level of negative thoughts, aim to cut them by at least half within a month by using the three techniques in this chapter. Keep on cutting them. You'll soon find that you silence them automatically.

Whether you think you can or whether you think you can't, you're right.

Henry Ford

● Total up your negative thoughts

4 Getting motivated

When you're feeling a bit **low** or, worse, **depressed**, it can be very difficult to motivate yourself. Because you feel demoralized you just can't get round to tackling anything. As a result, the problems mount and your sense of hopelessness increases. It's a downward spiral, but one you can get out of with the help of this chapter.

It's a downward spiral, but one you can get out of
....

In this section you'll be discovering both **behavioural** and **cognitive** techniques for overcoming inertia and apathy – and for increasing **motivation**. Here's your four-point plan:

1 Challenge your negative thinking.
2 Do *something* positive, no matter how small.
3 Make a plan and carry it out one step at a time.
4 Try enjoyment forecasting.

● It's important to overcome inertia

Challenge negative thinking

Negative thinking is at the root of inertia. CBT has various very effective methods for overcoming it.

The first is to employ the **three-column technique** (see Chapter 2) for exposing the distortions in your thinking.

Example of using the three-column technique for motivation

Negative thoughts	Distortions	Realistic thoughts
There's no point in looking for a job because I'm a loser and, in any case, there are no jobs	Labelling/ magnifying	I've succeeded in many things in the past. It's ridiculous to say that there are 'no jobs'. Most people have jobs and, if they can do it, so can I

Do something positive

Another way of tackling negative thoughts is to take some action, no matter how small. Just by **acting** you'll automatically elevate your mood.

This may seem to clash with pure cognitive therapy, which holds that **tackling thoughts** comes first. But this is the **behavioural** part of CBT and the two approaches reinforce one another. As all kinds of successful creative people know, it's pointless lying in bed waiting for inspiration. Far more effective is to sit down at that keyboard, or take up that paint brush, chisel or whatever and **begin**. You then benefit from:

* **positive reinforcement** (the pleasure of achievement)
* **negative reinforcement** (the end of feeling hopeless).

Make a plan

You may find it helpful to **plan your day**. Buy a **diary** and draw a line right down the middle of the page for that day. On the left-hand side note the things you'd **like to do**. For example, at 11 a.m. you might put 'Phone for job interview'. At bedtime enter what you actually did accomplish on the right-hand side. As the days go by, aim to **achieve more** and more of the things you planned.

Do

✔ *Do make your plan realistic but also as enjoyable as possible.*
✔ *Do reward yourself for every task you complete.*

Don't

✘ *Don't fill your plan with only hard work.*

One step at a time ...

Sometimes a task can seem so daunting that it seems pointless even trying to begin. The secret is to **focus on the first step** and nothing more.

CASE STUDY

Beatrice wanted to train as a ballet dancer. But after the first few lessons she was completely demoralized. The task ahead seemed so enormous. Then her teacher told her to take it literally just one step at a time. By focusing on the immediate task and getting it right Beatrice created a momentum and feeling of optimism that carried her through to a professional career.

The secret is to focus on the first step

* Select just **one task.**
* Break that task down into **manageable chunks.**
* Focus on the first chunk and get it done.
* **Congratulate yourself.**
* Move on to the next chunk.

Accomplishing the first chunk will give you a sense of **achievement** that will carry you to the next. If you still have a problem, make each chunk even smaller.

● Break that task down into manageable chunks

A journey of a thousand miles begins with one small step.

Chinese proverb

44

Enjoyment forecasting

When you feel low you often **jump to negative conclusions** about how much you might enjoy something. As a result, you don't do it.

The **enjoyment forecasting** technique can help.

In a notebook divide a page vertically. On the left-hand side write the name of something you might do, enter your thoughts on how enjoyable it might be and give it a score out of ten. Then go and do it.

Afterwards, on the right-hand side, enter how enjoyable it actually was and, again, give a score out of ten.

Most of the time you'll find you enjoyed the task or event more than you thought you would.

Example of the enjoyment forecasting technique

Forecast enjoyment	Actual enjoyment
Dinner party. Won't find anyone I get on with. Will be bored. Score 3	Met a very nice person. Exchanged details. Score 7
Jogging. Will be cold and legs will hurt. Score 4	Soon warmed up and felt quite exhilarated at the end. Score 8

CASE STUDY

Amanda was always finding reasons not to take part in the kinds of activities her friends enjoyed. Yet, if they insisted she come, she invariably did enjoy herself. When Amanda used the enjoyment forecasting technique she saw how negative and wrong her thoughts were.

An important part of motivation is simply to **think positively**. For example, if you wish to lose weight, first make a list of all the positive consequences of being slimmer. It might look like this:

* I'll feel more attractive.
* I'll be healthier.
* I'll be more active.
* I'll have more self-respect.

Just before going to sleep, **visualize** yourself as a slim person in a place you'd really love to be. For example, you might visualize yourself on a beautiful beach in the Caribbean. As you do so, go through your list, and say to yourself, 'Other people will find me attractive as they watch me preparing my surf board ...'

5 Handling criticism and self-criticism

There's no reason that any **criticism** anybody makes should ever upset you in the least. In fact, if you only realized it, the criticism of others never *has* upset you. It's the **negative thoughts** *you* have *after* hearing criticism that are upsetting, along with your own **self-criticism**.

There's no reason that any criticism anybody makes should ever upset you

It can be extremely difficult at first to accept the idea that other people's **criticisms** need not make you feel bad. But if you think about it for a while you'll realize that it's true.

In this chapter you'll learn how to identify and **correct the negative distortions** that follow criticism. For that you'll use:

* the three-column technique.

You'll also learn:

* how to **disarm** a critic
* how to recognize and deal with perfectionism
* how to recognize and deal with self-criticism.

If evil be spoken of you and it be true, correct yourself; if it be a lie, laugh at it.

Epictetus c. 55–135 CE, Greek Stoic philosopher

More uses of the three-column technique

The next time you receive a criticism, analyse your thoughts using the three-column technique. Let's say your boss has disregarded some recommendations you made in a report. Here's the three-column technique in action:

Example of dealing with criticism from your boss

Negative thoughts following criticism	Distortions	Realistic thoughts
By not implementing my recommendations he's showing that he considers my opinion to be worthless. I'll never get on. I'm a loser	All-or-nothing thinking/ generalizing/jumping to negative conclusions/ labelling	There could be all kinds of reasons for his failure to act. He might be afraid or incompetent

Criticism can be particularly **wounding** when it comes from someone close. Let's say your partner has expressed concern at the mounting unpaid bills. Your three-column entries might look like this:

Example of dealing with criticism from your partner

Negative thoughts following criticism	Distortions	Rational thoughts
Obviously my partner thinks I'm a failure and has lost respect for me. You can't love someone you don't respect. I *am* a failure. I'm unlovable	All-or-nothing thinking/ generalizing/jumping to negative conclusions/ magnifying/labelling	My partner is just worried. That's natural. In reality I receive plenty of love. Between us we can work out ways to save money and earn a bit extra

Disarm your critics

Of course, your options are not confined to accepting or ignoring criticism. If you think that the other person is wrong or has things out of proportion, then you can **put forward your own point of view**.

But you don't want the situation to escalate into a row. It's a common human response to become defensive when challenged and to stubbornly refuse to consider other ideas. The solution is first to **disarm** your critic.

54

● First try to disarm your critics

How does the disarmament process work?

There are three steps:

1 Ask for **clarification**. In other words, ask the other person to explain more fully why they're making the criticism. In this way you make sure you understand the criticism, demonstrate that you're willing to engage positively and, most important of all, force the other person to reconsider their position.
2 Seek **agreement**. Well, not necessarily with everything. But, if you can, find *something* to agree with. This will diffuse any anger or aggression on the other person's part.
3 Aim to **resolve** the situation through amicable discussion.

Perfectionism

Is anything that human beings do ever perfect?

☐ Yes.
☐ No.

If you answered 'yes', then you're not only wrong but you're also probably a **perfectionist** making yourself unhappy with **self-criticism**. And for no reason. Here's the test. If something is perfect, then it can't be improved on. Do you *really* believe that there are man-made things that can't be improved in *any* way?

Here we have to distinguish between aiming for perfection and aiming for a high standard. The two are not the same. As nothing human beings do is ever perfect, aiming for perfection is crippling and futile.

Aiming for perfection is crippling and futile

56

Try listing the **disadvantages** of your **perfectionism**. Here are some suggestions:

* I never finish anything on time.
* I'm afraid to try out new ideas in case I fail.
* Other people don't like working with me.
* I don't accomplish as much as other people.
* I can never take any satisfaction in anything I do.
* I make myself unhappy.

Another style of perfectionism is to visualize the perfect way you want things to be in the future. The wedding day is a classic example. But you'll be happier if you're more accepting of the way things are, rather than the way you'd like them to be.

Self-criticism

Do you often say things like this?

* I **should** be more successful.
* I **should** try harder for promotion.
* I **should** keep the house cleaner.
* I **should** have got a higher mark.

Attacking yourself with the 'should' word is often the result of comparing yourself too much with others. But we're all different, and what's right for other people is not necessarily right for you.

58

● Not everyone has to climb the promotion ladder

When you self-criticize with the 'should' word, ask yourself if it's really appropriate. Why should you try for promotion? Maybe you're happy in your present job. Maybe promotion would mean less time with your family. There are all kinds of reasons why promotion might not be the obvious step that it seems.

The best 'should' to remember is this:

✳ I should not say should.

A critic is a bundle of biases ...
Whitney Balliett

6 How to deal with anger

What's the best way to deal with **anger**:

* suppress it?
* express it?

People get good at the things they practise, and that includes anger. If you often get angry, then you'll simply become very good at getting angry. That applies whether you internalize your anger or whether you let it explode.

People get good at the things they practise, and that includes anger

The best thing, then, is not to get angry in the first place. Because anger can be a very **dangerous** emotion for everyone involved.

In this chapter you'll learn:

● Anger can be a very dangerous emotion

* how to change the **distorted thoughts** that lead to anger
* how to diffuse anger by:
  » being more **empathetic**
  » using **role playing** and **visualization** to prepare for difficult situations
  » introducing **cooling-off** periods.

Change the distorted thoughts that lead to anger

Think of a saucepan of milk on a stove. If you want to stop it boiling over, you could try putting the lid on more firmly. Or you could try taking the lid off altogether. But whichever of those two options you choose, the milk will still be boiling away. The best thing would be to **turn the heat down**.

Exactly the same thing applies to anger. Turn the heat down. Anger tends to build anger. Quite soon a point is reached at which emotions are completely out of control.

> **TOP TIP**
> No one can discuss matters rationally once their heart rate goes above 100 beats per minute – a condition known as 'flooding'.

How can you turn the heat down? In fact, you can do it simply by **changing your thoughts**, because:

✳ It's you who makes yourself angry, not outside events.

You may find this difficult to believe at first. After all, if someone does something terrible to you, it's normal to get angry, isn't it? Normal, yes. Helpful, probably not. Essential, no.

CASE STUDY

A carpenter had just completed laying a new floor. The householders were happily admiring it when the telephone rang. No one could find it. Then the carpenter realized that he had boarded it in under the floor. The husband was furious. But the wife laughed. Two different reactions.

It's all to do with those **distorted thoughts** again. But you could change them. Any or all of the ten distortions may be involved in anger, but the following four are especially significant:

1 jumping to negative conclusions
2 labelling
3 magnifying
4 'should' statements.

✳ **Jumping to negative conclusions** Involves imputing the worst motives when other people do things with which we strongly disagree. We say, 'He's doing that to make money.' Or, 'She's trying to make herself look important.' But, in fact, we usually don't know what another person's motives are.

* **Labelling** ('Scum' 'Sadist' 'Monster') Removes the need to consider the complexities of a situation. The person we're demonizing becomes a symbol for all the people we've been angry with in the past.
* **Magnifying** Means we exaggerate the significance and consequences of what's been said or done. For example, a man forgets his wife's birthday and she tells herself, 'That means he never loved me at all.'
* **'Should' statements** Often linked to unrealistic expectations, disappointments and anger. Examples are: 'I should have achieved more' and 'They should be more efficient.'

When you spot these distortions in your thinking, do your best to correct them.

Defusing anger

And here are five techniques for **defusing anger**:

1 upside/downside
2 role play
3 visualization

4 empathy
5 cooling-off period.

✳ **Upside/downside** is a simple method for comparing the advantages and disadvantages of a behaviour. On a sheet of paper make your upside/downside comparison like this:

Example of the upside/downside technique for controlling anger

Upside	Downside
People will know I'm not to be messed with I'll feel better for having my say	Others may become more aggressive I can have my say without getting angry but if I speak in anger I may say things I'll regret Getting angry is bad for my health

✻ **Role play** will allow you to practise remaining calm under provocation. No matter how much you resolve not to get angry, it's all too easy to get caught off guard by an unexpected situation. That's where this technique comes in. For role play you'll need the co-operation of a friend to attack your weak spots. For example:

Your friend: 'You're a terrible parent. Why don't you spend more time at home?'

You (**calmly**): 'You're right. I should spend more time with my children. And my partner. It's hard to balance those with work ...'

TOP TIP
Don't just read about role play. Really do it. Ask your friend to be as provocative as possible.

* **Visualization** works in the same way as role play but allows you to be far more flexible. You can imagine yourself remaining tranquil in all kinds of difficult situations and thus **program** yourself with that response. For example, visualize dealing calmly with a person who runs into your car.

* **Empathy** allows you to consider the situation from the other person's point of view. Before you speak or act just take the time to do that, and you may realize that what had seemed to be malicious or unfair wasn't at all.

Imagine yourself remaining tranquil in all kinds of difficult situations

* **Cooling-off** periods are useful not only in industrial relations but in life generally. The fact is that human beings can be so overcome by the build-up of 'anger chemicals' in the brain that they can no longer think and behave rationally. This is known as **flooding**. When you notice that you're close to flooding it's vital to stop arguing. Agree that you'll return to the subject (if necessary) on another occasion.

Anger is a short madness.
Horace

● Imagine yourself remaining tranquil

7 You're not a bad person

If you do something wrong, it would be appropriate to feel remorse. To say '**sorry**'. You can try to put the situation right and endeavour to make sure that it doesn't happen again. But for some people that isn't enough. They torture themselves with **guilt**. If that sounds like you, this chapter will help you to see that guilt is a crippling and pointless emotion.

Guilt is a crippling and pointless emotion
....

Here's the difference between remorse and guilt:

* Remorse makes you feel bad about what you've **done**.
* Guilt makes you feel bad about yourself as a **person**.

You're not a bad person because you did a bad thing. Good people can do bad things. In this chapter you'll learn how to **defeat guilt**, principally by using:

* the three-column technique.

Guilt

Here are some more questions to ask yourself:

* Do I deserve to suffer?
* If yes, what kind of suffering?
* If so, for how long?
* What happens when the self-inflicted punishment ends?

When you ask yourself these kinds of questions you begin to realize how **ridiculous** the whole notion of guilt is. There is nothing to be gained by feeling guilty.

Here's another question to ask yourself:

✷ Are my feelings of guilt **helpful** in any way?

In truth, guilt, like anger, is an emotion that benefits no one. If you feel guilty, you already know you did something wrong. So the guilt is **superfluous**. Worse, it probably paralyses you and prevents you acting rationally. When you're overcome by guilt it's difficult to behave **positively** and relate to other people in a normal way. No one will like you more because you feel guilty.

The man who makes no mistakes does not usually make anything.

Edward John Phelps

What causes guilt?

Any of the negative distortions described in Chapter 2 could be responsible for feelings of guilt. But these four are especially significant:

1 magnifying
2 personalizing
3 'should' statements
4 labelling.

Let's take a look at them in the context of guilt and see how the three-column technique can help.

No guilty man is acquitted if judged by himself.

Juvenal

Overcoming guilt

You may feel that you've done a terrible thing, but are you sure? Is it really as bad as you're making out? It could be that you're torturing yourself because you're magnifying the significance of what you've done. Use the three-column technique to provide some balance.

Using the three-column technique to overcome magnifying

Thoughts now	Distortions	Rational thoughts
I drove too fast, which means I could easily have killed a child who ran out, which means I'm no better than a murderer	Magnifying	Driving too fast is certainly wrong but it's not equivalent to killing someone deliberately. From now on I'll observe speed limits

It's nice to help people and normal to feel pleasure in doing so. But if you're often motivated by guilt and its avoidance then you're making the error of **personalizing**. That's to say, you're taking personal responsibility for things that aren't your responsibility.

Using the three-column technique to overcome personalizing

Thoughts now	Distortions	Rational thoughts
I should make my partner happy, and yet my partner isn't happy, so I must be at fault	Personalizing (and 'should' statement)	I do lots of things to make my partner happy and nothing to make my partner unhappy, so my partner's mood must be due to something else

Another form of personalizing is to feel guilt when **someone over-reacts** to something you've said. Ask yourself this:

✱ Are the other person's thoughts rational or distorted?

Let's say you criticize something your partner has done or said. Your partner then thinks like this, 'My partner doesn't respect me or love me and never has. It's clear we'll never be happy together.'

Your partner's thoughts themselves include the **distortions** of **jumping to negative conclusions** and **magnifying**. But *you* cannot be responsible for *your partner's* distorted thinking.

Are you constantly feeling guilty about your failure to do things you 'should' have done? Then you're making far too many **'should' statements**. Learn to challenge them with questions such as:

* Who says I should?
* Why should I?

Using the three-column technique to overcome 'should' statements

Thoughts now	Distortions	Rational thoughts
I should take care of my father myself. He would hate it in a home for the elderly If I don't, I'm a rotten daughter	Should statement (and personalizing/jumping to negative conclusions/ labelling)	He might enjoy the company in the home. He'll be well cared for

Most important of all is to stop giving yourself **negative labels**.

- ☑ All humans make mistakes.
- ☑ I'm a human, therefore I will make mistakes.
- ☑ I won't be hard on myself for being human.
- ☑ Doing something bad doesn't make me a bad person.

Using the three-column technique to overcome labelling

Thoughts now	Distortions	Rational thoughts
I'm evil because I have erotic fantasies about my best friend's partner	Labelling	Just about everyone has those kinds of fantasies – they mean I'm normal

8 Building happiness on solid foundations

We all feel happier when nice things happen to us. Of course we do. But it's a mistake to rely *exclusively* on external things for joy and self-worth. **Happiness** built entirely on **externals** is a happiness built on **shaky** foundations. If you depend on status or on the appreciation, respect and love of others, then you're following a common but risky strategy.

Happiness built entirely on externals is a happiness built on shaky foundations

Think about it for a moment. If your partner were to leave you tomorrow, could you *never* be happy on your own? Or if you were to get the sack tomorrow, would you somehow be worth less as a person than you are now?

Things such as employment, appreciation and love are not totally within your control. In this chapter we'll be establishing your **happiness** and **self-worth** on something that *is.* Your thinking. We'll be using the following techniques:

* upside/downside
* enjoyment forecasting
* self-praise.

Happiness and self-worth

See how many of these statements you agree with. In order to have a
sense of self-worth and be happy it's essential:

☐ to have someone special to share things with
☐ to be loved
☐ to have a good job
☐ to be respected by other people.

All of these things are nice. No one is arguing with that. But are they
essential to happiness? If you think they are, then you're **denying**
yourself the possibility of happiness should you, for whatever reason, be
without one or more of them.

Let's turn things round and look at them from a different direction. Do you know any people who are:

- ☐ unhappy even though they have good jobs and are respected
- ☐ unhappy even though they are loved by one or more people
- ☐ happy even though they live alone
- ☐ happy even though other people look down on them as weird or eccentric?

If you ticked those boxes you have the proof that happiness and self-worth need to be rooted **inside** you.

The summit of happiness is reached when a person is ready to be what he is.

Erasmus

The upside/downside technique

The idea that your happiness and your self-worth can be independent of how much you are loved or respected may at first seem perverse. Let's examine the notion using the **upside/downside** technique.

Divide a sheet of paper vertically. On the left-hand side enter the advantages of thinking that self-worth depends on love and respect. On the right-hand side enter the disadvantages. You'll almost certainly find that the downside far outweighs the upside.

● You can be happy on your own

Using the upside/downside technique to determine the basis of happiness and self-worth

Upside	Downside
When people admire me it feels nice and proves the value of what I've done	If I rely on other people's admiration that means I can't derive any satisfaction from things they don't admire I'll be afraid to be unorthodox
If someone loves me, that means my life has a point	If I depend on love to give my life meaning, that means that nothing else has any meaning

TOP TIP
The upside/downside technique can be used for all sorts of dilemmas. Try it whenever you're not sure what to do.

Enjoyment forecasting

Let's try to tackle your belief that another human being is essential to your happiness by using the **enjoyment forecasting** technique.

In a notebook divide a page vertically. On the left-hand side describe something you might do, enter your thoughts on how enjoyable it might be if you were alone and give it a score out of ten. Then go and do it on your own. Afterwards, on the right-hand side, enter how enjoyable it actually was on your own and, again, give a score out of ten.

Life isn't about finding yourself.
Life is about creating yourself.

George Bernard Shaw

Using the enjoyment forecasting technique for evaluating being alone

Forecast enjoyment	Actual enjoyment
Hiking. The views will be meaningless without someone to share them with. Score 3	Spectacular scenery that I stopped to sketch whenever I wanted. Score 7
Preparing a special Italian meal. What's the point? Score 2	I was able to have everything exactly the way I like it. Score 6

Most of the time you'll find that you enjoyed the activity on your own far more than you thought you would. Indeed, there are certain things that, quite often, you'll enjoy *more* on your own.

Self-praise

We all like to receive praise. But rather than rely on the praise of others, why not go in for some **self-praise**?

Do any of the following apply to you?

- ☐ When I review things I've done I tend to **minimize** my achievements and **magnify** my mistakes.
- ☐ When I review things I've done I tend to focus on what went **wrong** rather than on what went **right.**
- ☐ If other people don't praise what I've done I believe it's no good.

If you ticked one or more of those you need to be more complimentary about yourself.

Here's how to replace the compliments of others with your own.

✱ Be on the lookout for anything you do well, no matter how insignificant. Praise yourself.
✱ Review the past to identify anything you've already done well, no matter how insignificant. Praise yourself.
✱ Make a daily tally in a notebook, in the memo facility of a mobile phone or on a wrist counter. Every day, total up the number of praiseworthy things. Make certain your score increases every day. Keep this up until self-praise has become an automatic habit.

Be on the lookout for anything you do well, no matter how insignificant

9 Fears, phobias and obsessions

Most of us have at least one **irrational fear**, or a **phobia**, or an **obsessive** type of behaviour. It might be a fear of heights or spiders, for example, or a phobia about dirt, or an obsessive need to keep everything in order. CBT has **powerful techniques** for dealing with all these kinds of things.

Most of us have at least one irrational fear

....

Those of us with unwarranted fears, phobias and obsessions can usually live our lives quite happily by avoiding difficult situations. But sometimes the feelings become so overwhelming that life is miserable. The CBT approach incorporates:

* **relaxation** exercises
* **desensitization** through **gradual exposure**
* correcting cognitive **distortions**.

Do the thing you are afraid to do, and the death of fear is certain.

Ralph Waldo Emerson

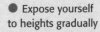

● Expose yourself to heights gradually

Relax ...

The first step is to learn some **relaxation techniques** so you can apply them during the gradual exposure.

It has been proven that, if you can manage to control your breathing and **exhale** for **longer** than you inhale, then you can induce a feeling of relaxation and **tranquility**.

* Close your eyes and focus on your **breathing**.
* Count up to **7** as you breathe in and **11** as you breathe out.
* Continue like this, gradually extending your inhalations and exhalations but always preserving the same 7:11 ratio.
* You can increase the effect by touching your fingertips together and making a 'steeple' of your hands over your stomach.

Here's another relaxation technique:

* Close your eyes and imagine that you're holding a **balloon** just in front of your face.
* Exhale gently and steadily into the balloon and let your hands move apart as it inflates.
* Inhale, sucking air out of the balloon and letting your hands move closer together.

TOP TIP
If you're actually overcome by a panic attack and become faint, hold a **paper bag** over your nose and mouth so you're **rebreathing** your own breath. This will **normalize** the carbon dioxide level in your blood and stop you feeling lightheaded.

Desensitization

Now you're ready for **desensitization** through **gradual exposure**. This is the behavioural part of CBT. Gradual exposure can overcome all kinds of fears, from spiders to public speaking. Let's see how it works for a fear of water.

1 **Relax** on the side of the pool with your feet skimming the water
2 **Relax** on the ladder or steps with your ankles in the water
3 **Relax** on the ladder or steps with the water above your knees
4 Continue in the same way until you're able to immerse your head.

Gradual exposure can overcome all kinds of fears

Some tips:

* If you feel alarmed, go back to the previous stage at which you felt comfortable and use your relaxation techniques. Once you feel calm, try again.
* If you still feel fearful, return to a stage at which you feel happy, enjoy it, and then stop for the day.
* You don't have to achieve everything in one session. You can continue the process over several days or even weeks.
* Never attempt to do it all in one go, or let anyone push you 'in at the deep end'. That will only make things worse. *Gradual* exposure is the key.

Cognitive distortions

Behavioural therapy alone may be enough but sometimes it's helpful to add in **cognitive therapy**. Refer back to the list of distorted ways of thinking in Chapter 2. There you will see five that particularly apply to irrational fears:

* focusing on the negative
* ignoring the positive
* labelling
* magnifying
* emotional reasoning.

● Try not to magnify problems

Do

✔ Do be **positive** about what you <u>can</u> do (for example, 'I'm a person who can stand in water up to my chest.').

Don't

✘ Don't focus on the **negative** by giving yourself a **label** (for example, 'afraid of water').

✘ Don't dwell on and **magnify** fears (for example, if you're afraid of heights, never imagine yourself falling to the ground below).

✘ Don't indulge in **emotional reasoning** (for example, 'I feel frightened, therefore the risk of falling off this building must be real.').

Men are disturbed not by things but by the view they take of them.

Epictetus

Desensitization for OCD

The desensitization process also works in a very similar way for **obsessive–compulsive disorder (OCD)**. In this context, obsessions are:

* intrusive and upsetting thoughts, images or impulses that persist even though the sufferer recognizes them as irrational.

Compulsions are:

* repetitive behaviours provoked by or linked to the obsessions.

Anxiety is considered to be at the root of OCD. In some cases there is a connection between the obsession and the compulsion. For example:

* an exaggerated fear of germs may lead to excessive hand washing.

In other cases there is no logic at all:

* counting steps or cracks in the pavement.

In behavioural therapy, the specific style of desensitization for OCD is sometimes known as **exposure and response prevention** (ERP). For example, if you have a **phobia** about dirt, an obsession about cleanliness, and consequently a compulsion to wash your hands frequently, you would gradually accustom yourself to dirt with little or no hand washing. The stages might be:

1 shaking hands with various people
2 looking at second-hand books
3 pulling up weeds in the garden
4 using a public toilet
5 cleaning a toilet.

Remember, you must only permit the compulsive behaviour (in this case hand washing) if there's a genuine need and, then, **only once**.

10 Depression and suicidal thoughts

When something upsetting has happened it's perfectly normal to grieve and feel sad. But **depression** is something quite **different** from **sadness**.

Here, for example, are two kinds of response to the death of a loved one.

- ☑ Healthy response: 'I shall miss the love and companionship we had together.'
- ☒ Unhealthy response: 'I'll never be happy again. I'm nothing without him/her. I might as well be dead.'

Depression is something quite different from sadness

···

Episodes of depression usually come to an end quite naturally. But the average time is **eight months.** It could be shorter but it could also be longer. That's a long time to suffer. And sometimes depression gets worse, not better. So **prompt treatment** is essential. In this chapter we'll look at:

* how to recognize depression
* the different kinds of depression
* some additional treatments for depression
* what to do if you have suicidal feelings.

How to recognize depression

Ask yourself how many of the following realistically justify depression:

☐ divorce
☐ bankruptcy
☐ unemployment
☐ serious illness

☐ physical disability
☐ old age
☐ death of someone close.

How many did you tick? If you ticked any at all, then you were wrong. The proof is that many people experience these things **without being depressed**. Depression stems from **distortions** in thinking.

The difference between sadness and depression

Sadness	Depression
Realistic thinking	Distorted thinking
Naturally ends fairly soon	Persists for a long time or recurs
Doesn't involve loss of self-worth	Always involves loss of self-worth

If you're not sure whether you have **depression**, tick the items on this list that apply to you:

- ☐ constant sadness
- ☐ constant fatigue with no apparent physical cause
- ☐ loss of self-confidence and self-esteem
- ☐ feelings of hopelessness and helplessness
- ☐ finding no pleasure in anything, including sex
- ☐ sleep problems
- ☐ inability to concentrate.

Depression can range from **mild** through **moderate** to **major** (clinical). One or two ticks could be owing to various things, but, if you ticked three or more items, then you're probably depressed. The more items you ticked the more serious your depression.

The chain of thoughts

Constructing a **chain of thoughts** is a way of probing deeper and deeper into your own mind. It works in a very simple way. Divide a sheet of paper into three columns. Head up the left-hand column 'Negative thoughts', the middle-column 'Distortions' and the right-hand column 'Realistic thoughts'. After filling in your first upsetting thought follow the chain by asking yourself *why* that thought is upsetting, and then why *that* thought is upsetting, and so on. The aim is to discover the fundamental distortion that lies at the bottom of everything.

To love oneself is the beginning of a lifelong romance.

Oscar Wilde

Example of a chain of thoughts

Negative thoughts	Distortions	Realistic thoughts
My partner criticized something I did		
That means my partner doesn't love and respect me	All-or-nothing thinking/ magnifying/jumping to negative conclusions	Criticism of something I did is not criticism of me as a person
That means I'm pathetic	Generalizing/focusing on the negative	I'm not pathetic
That means we're bound to break up	Jumping to negative conclusions	Disagreeing about something does not mean separating is either desirable or likely
That means I'll be unhappy because I'll be alone	Jumping to negative conclusions	Other people are happy alone and I could be, too

What triggers depression?

It may help if you can analyse your behaviour to see if you can discover what **triggers** your depression and what helps lift you out of it. Ask yourself:

✻ What happens just before the depression?
✻ What happens during the depression?
✻ What happens as the depression lifts?

In this way you may be able to uncover the kinds of incidents that unleash your depression and maintain it, as well as the thoughts or actions that defeat it. If so, make the necessary changes in your behaviour.

SAD

Seasonal affective disorder (SAD) is a special category of depression triggered by a lack of sunshine in winter. The three possible treatments are:

* trying to change your **thinking** so that gloomy weather no longer provokes gloomy thoughts
* using a SAD **light box** that mimics natural sunlight
* taking an extended **holiday** where the days are longer and the **sun** more constant – or even emigrating, if possible.

Note that, if you buy a SAD light box, you'll need to keep it on for several hours a day. Typical models produce a light intensity of 2,500–10,000 lux, compared with 100,000 lux for the real thing in summer.

Other treatments for depression

CBT can be used in conjunction with **antidepressants** prescribed by a doctor. **Exercise** naturally increases the level of the body's own antidepressants, including:

* **endorphins** (morphine-like substances) that combat pain and promote happiness
* **phenylethylamine (PEA)**, the substance responsible for the euphoria of a new romance
* **noradrenaline** (also known as norepinephrine), which increases positivity and expansiveness.

About **20–30 minutes** of vigorous exercise every other day can be as effective as antidepressant tablets.

Exercise naturally increases the level of the body's own antidepressants

118

Warning signs

Don't rely on self-administered CBT alone if any of the following apply to you:

- ☐ self-harm
- ☐ the feeling that there was never a time in your life when you were happy
- ☐ the feeling that you never could be happy
- ☐ the feeling that suicide is the only solution
- ☐ working out a plan to commit suicide
- ☐ a history of suicide attempts.

If you scored one or more ticks you should seek professional help immediately.

Believe that life is worth living and your belief will help create the fact.

William James

Other books by the author

Be More Confident (Teach Yourself, Hodder Education, 2010).

Transform Your Life with NLP (Teach Yourself, Hodder Education, 2010).

How To Be Happier (Teach Yourself, Hodder Education, 2010).

Beat Your Depression (Hodder Arnold, 2007).

Help Yourself To Live Longer (Teach Yourself, Hodder Education, 2010).

Master the Art of Confidence (Flash, Hodder Education, 2011).

Kickstart Your Life with NLP (Flash, Hodder Education, 2011).